Is Your Networking Net Working?

IS YOUR
Networking Net
Working?

**The How To Guide for Professionals and
Entrepreneurs to Become Their Own
Center of Influence**

JOHN R. DADE

NEW YORK

LONDON • NASHVILLE • MELBOURNE • VANCOUVER

Is Your Networking Net Working?

The How to Guide for Professionals and Entrepreneurs to Become Their Own Center of Influence

Published in New York, New York, by Morgan James Publishing. Morgan James is a trademark of Morgan James, LLC. www.MorganJamesPublishing.com

The Morgan James Speakers Group can bring authors to your live event. For more information or to book an event visit The Morgan James Speakers Group at www.TheMorganJamesSpeakersGroup.com.

ISBN 9781642790474 paperback
ISBN 9781642790481 eBook
Library of Congress Control Number: 2018939795

Cover & Interior Design by:
Chris Treccani
www.3dogcreative.net

Cover Illustration by:
Nick Kirkland

In an effort to support local communities, raise awareness and funds, Morgan James Publishing donates a percentage of all book sales for the life of each book to Habitat for Humanity Peninsula and Greater Williamsburg.

Get involved today! Visit www.MorganJamesBuilds.com

To my beautiful wife and best friend Lydia who suggested that I write this book and who was patient and understanding as I started, stalled, procrastinated, and then finally got to it and finished.

Thank you ... and I love you!

TABLE OF CONTENTS

ACKNOWLEDGMENTS

Just as networking can't be done alone, I quickly discovered that writing a book is not a one man endeavor either! This book would not have happened without a great group of friends and mentors who came to my rescue early on. To all of them I owe a huge thank you!

David Rohlander... my friend and mentor. An accomplished author (*The CEO Code, Idiot's Guide to Management Skills*), speaker, and corporate trainer who inspired me to actually start putting words on paper and also enlightened me in his wise and fatherly way that "putting words together is the easy part. Making it into a book that people want to read is where the work begins!" A truth to be sure.

W. Terry Whalen ... the acquisitions editor at Morgan James Publishing whose guidance and patience through our many conversations consisting of my asking a myriad of first-time writer questions that he calmly answered while giving me the confidence to keep going and do it properly. Morgan James Publishing, it's Founder, David Hancock and his entire team who held my hand through the entire "publishing" process and are the reason my thoughts made it to print and to the public. A Very Sincere Thank You!

The Cigar Night Business Mixer Group and the original members who joined me and stayed on board and dedicated their time and energy to make the CNBMG the success it is today. Thank you, Nick Kirkland, Sergey Molkov, Paul Fernandez, and Jevon Thomas.

And also to those who started and manage their own CNBMG Chapters in San Diego: Chaz Dykes, Renee Palermo, Randy Rodriguez, Nowell Wisch, and Christopher Walters. In Los Angeles: Sandip Thiary, Brian Nguyen, Shawana Isaac, Erik Berliner, and Yvonne Morris.

And finally, a huge thank you to all the many great cigar and spirits vendors who supported our

CNBMG efforts and enhanced our networking mixers from the beginning, especially my cigar reps: CigarMan Andy Scharfman, Casey Aldulaimi, DonJuan Gross, Ron Wagner, Shervin Fazeliaref, Hollywood Jose Morel, Alex and Tony "The Cigar Guys," and Ribhi "Robbie" Saoud, owner of the Vintage Cigar Lounge where it all started.

My spirits reps: Ricardo Gamarra, German Gonzalez, Johnny the Scott, Jon Trainer, April Gallegos, Mitch Bechard, Brandon Bartlett, and so many others. Thank you all!

PREFACE

Unless you change how you are, you will always have what you've got.

Jim Rohn
AMERICAN ENTREPRENEUR AND AUTHOR

The old adage, "It's not what you know, but who you know" is as true today as the day it was first coined. In addition, I would propose that it's not only who you know, but "who knows you!" We've all heard that knowledge is power. But I believe it's powerful only if you can get that knowledge about what you do to the people who need your product or service.

This is true whether you're in sales, own a restaurant or auto repair shop, or paint houses. And here's why. Like it or not, we're all salespeople! Whether we're interviewing for a job, talking to our boss about our next raise, or asking that special person for a date, we're selling.

We're selling either ourselves, or a product, or a service 24/7. Add to that the fact that in our internet world, knowledge and all matter of information is a mouse click away. So unfortunately, you or your product or service is just one of millions of things out there clamoring for the world's attention.

But here's the good news. *You* are unique! Only *you* can do what you do and offer it in the way you do.

So how do you get your message—your knowledge of what you do or offer—out there? This is the challenge I and many others in my profession faced in 2009. While the internet and traditional marketing tools worked well for certain products such as music or books, or for certain professions such as electrical contractors or dance instructors, my career in the alternative investment arena prevented me from using many of these accepted promotional and advertising avenues to get my message out there to my target audience—not to mention that my target prospect and potential client is probably not the type to spend his or her time surfing Facebook or Meetup sites.

In addition, my financial strategies were not necessarily appropriate for the mass population or casual investor. What's more, what many of us have experienced in the last several years, especially in the financial services field, is a shift to a need for more personal relationships among investors. This is even more so among my target market, the affluent, high net worth investor.

Given the niche investment area I specialize in, this relationship building has grown even more critical. In my earlier career in the restaurant industry, traditional networking avenues like Chamber of Commerce, business expo, and civic group events worked well because I was looking to attract members of the general population who had $10 or $20 to spend on food and drinks at my restaurants. I also did a lot of networking then and it worked fine.

When I made the transition to the financial arena and my target prospect was the upper 10 percent of the wealthy investor market, traditional methods simply didn't work. This sector of the population frequented the resort-style golf courses in the region, were members of exclusive clubs and groups, and typically weren't visitors at the local Chamber breakfast. I needed to find a way to meet these people and build relationships with them and their peers to achieve success in my career.

Hence the reason for creating my unusual marketing strategy through a unique networking format—it has helped me build lasting personal relationships and has accelerated my business and career growth while having a lot of fun along the way.

My wish is that you find in these pages inspiration, motivation, and bits of gold that you can use on your journey to solid business and personal relationships, more and better business, and more enjoyment in your life.

CHAPTER ONE

I'M STUCK!

*In a chronically leaking boat,
energy devoted to changing vessels is
more productive than energy devoted to
patching leaks.*

Warren Buffett
CEO OF BERKSHIRE HATHAWAY

I'm stuck! I'm frustrated! I've got to make a change!

These were my thoughts in late 2009 as the financial markets were bottoming out and faith and trust in them was at an all-time low.

I recall thinking to myself—hey, I have a great financial strategy with a long history of positive data and I'm good at what I do and knowledgeable about my product. I believe in my product and I'm very good at presenting it to those interested. So what was the problem?

I couldn't find enough qualified people to share it with.

All of this was running through my head (again!) as I made my 207th cold call during my routine work day.

Later that night, I vented to my group of friends after work as we gathered for our twice-weekly cigar session at our local cigar lounge. That's when I saw a commonality emerging. We were all bitching about the same thing. This was not a "woe is me pity party." It was a conversation among driven professionals searching for a better and more productive way to grow our business. The weird thing was ... we all had different occupations: a CPA, an insurance agent, a guy who did custom home remodeling, and a financial advisor.

When one of the group asked me, "Who's your client and what does your best prospect look like?" I responded automatically with, "They're generally high net worth individuals who are open to looking at new investment strategies." That's when a group-think moment happened, and we all decided to try a modified Ben Franklin approach to solving our problem.

So we grabbed some paper and pens and asked these questions and jotted down the answers:

Questions:

Who was our target prospect?

What do they do?

What are their hobbies?

Where do they spend their down time?

Answers:

Age 35-65, $500,000-5 million net worth

Professionals, executives, business owners

Cars, boats, golf, fine dining /spirits, cigars

Private clubs, golf resorts, traveling

Since I didn't play golf, that was out. So I decided to meet them at the 19th hole! That discussion and list led to the formation of a unique and smokin' type of business networking format.

The Cigar Night Business Mixer Group was born!

CHAPTER TWO

THE "AHA" MOMENT

Ideas are a **dime a dozen**. *People who implement them are priceless.*

Mary Kay Ash
FOUNDER OF MARY KAY COSMETICS

If you're in sales or any business where you need to meet more prospects, you already know that you need to network, make calls, and keep your pipeline full. And you know how frustrating it can be. If you're not a people person or an extrovert, you also know how challenging it can be in a networking event environment.

Early in my career as a financial professional, I attended professional groups, business referral groups, and open call large mixer groups, all without success. And with many of the closed groups that I was invited to and attended, you had to pay a start-up fee and monthly dues to join and refer business only to the people in the group. Add to that the fact that their meetings were so structured they were more work than my real work. While some found these groups beneficial, I found them restrictive ... and they just didn't work for me.

I will also add that in my area of business, the financial arena, as well as other professional areas such as banking, real estate, insurance, law, and accounting, events are held that are billed as training and networking opportunities. I've been to a number of these. They tend to be dry, instructional, technical, and, quite frankly, boring.

The same goes for seminars and workshops. These are good for the industry content they deliver, but they're not a very viable networking tool. Those attending are usually there because they have to be for continuing education hours or because they want be exposed to the information presented—not to network. In my opinion, many of these events actually seem primarily for the benefit of the organizer.

What's more, these events aren't structured for you to bring clients or potential clients along. So you end up seeing the same group of your peers, who are all talking shop to people in the same business.

Now, I wasn't always the outgoing, people person or social animal that I am today. But when it came to talking about my hobbies or what I liked to do, even in my early years I could go on and on and get quite animated. And these days I can hold a conversation with almost anyone in almost any setting. Yet I found that in most business networking environments, even getting a conversation started was daunting.

See if this sounds familiar. You're headed into the room where the "Who & What" Mixer/ Networking event is being held. You followed the standard mixer/networking rule—get there early and leave late—and there are a few people milling around. You walk up to a group of three people who are talking, and you're not acknowledged. You wait patiently for the opportunity to jump in and introduce yourself, then finally just say, "Hello, I'm John. How is everyone?" After a cool few seconds, you get a hello from each person, and then they all go back to their conversation. Maybe you get a "welcome" or a "good to meet you." So you stand there for a bit before you walk away and try again.

In the meantime, the room starts filling up and you're approached every few minutes by: "Hi. I'm Bob. Here's my card. What do you do? I sell widgets," and they proceed to spend the next twenty minutes trying to sell you. Then you get interrupted by another "sales" person, and as the event winds down, you're fatigued, you have sixty business cards—and zero prospects!

If that does sound familiar, you're not alone.

So picture this. First close your eyes for a few seconds.

Okay. You enter a networking event of fifty-plus people. You're greeted and welcomed by many of them and get the "nod" from a bunch more, you shake some hands, hug a few people, and they start talking with you about your passion or hobby. The next thing you know, two hours have passed, you've met a couple of dozen new people and have four to five appointments to meet over coffee, breakfast, or a drink with quality people you've chosen to follow up with.

Now take a moment and think about what just happened. Feels good, huh? Would that work for you? It could as the leader of your own networking group. It has for hundreds of our group's members. And I firmly believe it can for you as well.

You see, we humans are a curious and exploring bunch. We're always looking for a new experience. And when we discover a group of others who are like-minded and enjoy the experience with us and find value in being part of a group, we tend to not only return but tell others and invite them. And when it's your event, all those attending are potential clients and customers!

CHAPTER THREE

IF YOU BUILD IT, THEY WILL COME

If you don't belong to a private club, create your own.

Harvey Mackay
BESTSELLING AUTHOR AND BUSINESS GURU

This now famous line from the baseball movie *Field of Dreams* speaks volumes to me.

And when applied to networking, I believe it can work wonders.

Here's a diamond in the rough idea: You think you're not a good networker? Then by all means start networking, *your* way!

So how do you begin to network your way? How do you build a solid business networking group that benefits both you and its members?

First off, know that it should be fun, not work, so be prepared to loosen up and have a good time. Yes, there's a bit of work involved, but it should be enjoyable work. After all, it's about you—your hobby, your passion, and your business growth.

To get you started, here are a few items for you to consider:

1. Find your target market/prospect. Then define your prospect: who they are, what they like, and where they spend their down time.

2. Which passion do you want to build on? (I chose cigars and booze.) Your passion might be classic cars, wines, or ancient coins. What's more, while every hobby or passion may not lend itself to this type of networking format, if you give it some thought, you may discover

one you enjoy that could be utilized in some form as a vehicle for business networking.

3. Who can help you get started? You'll need to build a team. They should have shared interests and a desire for more business.

4. Don't talk business at these mixers unless someone insists. Discussion of business should happen in a natural and casual manner.

5. Don't pay for venues. This is our general rule. Except when we do!

The only exceptions to not paying for our venue is when we book at a private country club or members-only club such as the Grand Havana Room in Beverly Hills or the Center Club in Costa Mesa in Orange County, California. These usually have a set fee that is non-negotiable even for their own members' use of the facility.

For these mixers, we usually charge a small fee to attend to cover the costs. Our members are fine with these occasional upscale events and costs and enjoy these special venue mixers because of the opportunity to visit these unique locations. We also build in great value by having a spirits tasting vendor and cigar vendor join us, and we also provide appetizers to make the mixer a memorable event.

As you experiment with different venues, you'll find some that you don't care for. Other venues may not want your group back for whatever reason. But that's fine—there should be enough venues that do want your business. That was our experience, and along the way, we persisted and grew.

Perhaps the most important tip is to keep your mixers fun, loosely structured, and interesting.

Below is the overview of the format of our mixer group; the information is included in an email that is sent to those who inquire about starting their own chapter of a Cigar Night Business Mixer Group (CNBMG):

- Members are reminded to bring a spare cigar for an exchange.
- If the mixer is held at a cigar lounge, those who are attending need to buy there. It's important to support the venue. If the mixer is held elsewhere, attendees can bring their own cigars. Note that some of our venues are BYOB as well.
- Typically, our mixers begin at 5:30 p.m.
- You should have a sign-up sheet ready for those who come without business cards. Other attendees should leave their cards with the organizer at the front table.
- You may also want to offer raffle tickets. The money from the raffle can be used to buy a gift certificate from the venue ($20-$25 each, depending on how much money is collected). You can have two or more drawings depending on the amount of money collected, which supports the venue.

- Midway through the mixer, around 7 p.m., introduce yourself and have everyone give a ten-second "hello and here's what I do" pitch. Make sure to keep this time to ten seconds.
- Draw a business card for a thirty-second business pitch (and hold it to thirty seconds.)
- When it's time for the exchange, attendees go up to people they haven't met already, introduce themselves, and exchange cigars. It's a way to "stir up" the mixer.
- That's it for the formalities—everyone is then just invited to network and enjoy the evening.

Later in the week following the mixer, copies of business cards and the sign-up sheet go to the venue as another perk for its business.

CHAPTER FOUR

SO NOW WHAT? AND WHERE?

The secret of getting ahead is getting started. The secret to getting started is breaking your complex overwhelming tasks into small manageable tasks, and then starting on the first one.

Mark Twain

Finding a venue for your new networking group can be easier than you might think. But first you need to figure out what type of event you want to have and what hobby or passion you want to build it around. Is it coin collecting? Stamps? Books? Firearms? Cigars? Scotch?

Once decided, now what? Will there be food involved? Snacks? Full meals? Or just refreshments? Will there be wine, beer, or spirits? Who pays for what?

Will you need tables, chairs, or a podium? Will it be inside or outside? A quiet space, a private venue, or a public area? A restaurant, tavern, or pub? Will you need Wi-Fi, electricity, heat, air conditioning, a sound system or microphone, a video screen? Will it be the same venue each time or will it change each month or quarter?

Here are a few suggestions based on our seven years of hosting these mixer events on a monthly basis. Since we like to encourage mingling and networking we usually have only a few tables (preferably high tops) and a few chairs or seating areas. The venues work with us on the set-up. This creates a stand-up-and walk-around environment and helps keep the attendees in motion.

We also ask the venue to extend their Happy Hour menus or put together a special limited choice menu for our mixers, which they usually have no problem doing. If the mixer is held at a cigar lounge, we also ask for a multi-purchase discount, such as a promotion to buy three cigars and get one free or some other special pricing for our group that night. Again, the venue usually is happy to help.

Once these details are addressed and settled on, you're ready to pitch the venue. So here's an important point. Make it about *them*! Yes, right now you need the venue more than they need you. But pitch it properly and they *will* want your group and will work to bring you back.

As you know, the Cigar Night Business Mixer Group was built around my and the members' passion for premium cigars and spirits.

When I first approached the venues' managers or owners with only eight or so members, I didn't have a lot of leverage or resources to work with. Knowing that, I pitched any benefit I could think of that I could bring to the venue. I knew the venue would want to know how many people would be there so I volunteered that we could expect ten or more this time, that we were a new group, and that we were growing.

I also shared that I would bring *new* business consisting of business owners, executives, and professionals to their location on a slow night— people who would buy cigars, drinks, and food. I would promote their venue on social media sites and to our members' email base weekly starting three weeks before the mixer and a week after it, including photos and the venue location and logo. I would buy a gift certificate from the venue from our raffle money proceeds to raffle off. And finally, the venue would get a list of the attendees for their own promotional use. Then I'd share with them that I'd ask nothing in return except the use of their location for our mixers.

At this point, some venues became wary and asked why I would do all of this and want nothing in return from them? My answer was simple. My group wanted to support the venues that supported the cigar lifestyle and wanted our CNBMG group as customers.

Yes, the first six months of monthly cigar mixers were challenging—we only had a couple of locations that said "yes" and only a few attendees who showed up regularly. In addition, our format was to change venues each month so that they were exposed to our group more than a few times during the year.

By the end of the first year, we averaged twenty-plus attendees at each mixer. We also added a raffle and sold tickets and used the funds to buy more raffle prizes, which included gift certificates to the hosting venue. We then refined our mixer format to include a brief formal introduction session.

As we grew, venues started to take notice and were actually starting to call me to offer their locations for our mixers. Also, as we grew and were able to bring more value to the venues, I started to search for more upscale locations to add more prestige to our Cigar Mixer group and attract even more quality members.

Now, six years later, CNBMG has chapters in Orange County, Los Angeles, and San Diego. This growth was due to the success of our original Orange County group that attracted people from those areas and liked what we were doing and wanted to duplicate it in their own area.

And here's the fun part. Not a week goes by without a new venue calling and wanting to host our group at their location. And we don't pay for venues (except on rare occasions at exclusive private clubs.) That's because we've changed our pitch a bit. They now know we'll bring fifty to eighty-plus members who are professionals, executives, and business owners to their location who will eat, drink and buy cigars (if offered) and who will be exposed to their business. And we'll promote their location with photos and their logo to more than 2,000 members in our email base as well as through our extensive Facebook and LinkedIn following. In addition, at the event we'll purchase $50 or more in gift certificates from the venue to raffle off at the mixer that night. And finally, they'll receive a list of attendees for their promotional use.

These new selling points give value to the group and bring value to the venue. The venue in return does nothing extra nor is asked for anything extra. All we ask for is a place for our group to gather and network with fellow cigar and spirits enthusiasts.

CHAPTER FIVE

KEEP IT EXCLUSIVE BUT INCLUSIVE

Be a yardstick of quality.Some people aren't used to an environment where excellence is expected.

Steve Jobs
CO-FOUNDER OF APPLE

Okay, I will admit that I don't know who your target prospect is. But I hope that you do. If not, *now* is the time to stop and give it some serious thought. After all, it is your career.

I was fortunate that I did know my target prospect. My goal then became how to attract more of these people and get in front of them to share my product.

So how did I keep my CNBMG group exclusive to ensure the quality of the members, ones who I could do business with? By adhering to my quality over quantity strategy.

Yes, it was a challenge, but it can be done. Remember, you and your group members want the same outcome—a large, ever-changing group of quality people they can do business with and refer business to. So have them help you.

How? By sharing your vision and strategy with your group members—asking them to be part of the vision, getting their input, and asking them to share that vision with other quality people they know.

Let them know you're looking for quality over quantity. You're looking to attract professionals like *them*: people who know the value of building relationships versus making a quick sale. People who enjoy sharing their hobby and passion others who share that passion in a business casual, non-sales atmosphere while engaging in that hobby and passion.

Also share with your group members that integrity and professionalism are at the core of the mixer group's agenda. Once they understand and embrace your shared mission, they'll become your best ambassadors.

At this point I believe I need to interject an important disclaimer. While you might think that our choice of cigars and spirits as the theme for our networking mixers targets or attracts only men, you may be surprised to learn that there are many ladies who enjoy these passions as well.

Our Cigar Night Business Mixer Group has a wonderful following of ladies who are lawyers, realtors, caterers, and business owners of all types who join us regularly at our monthly events at all three of our CNBMG chapters. Some come as guests of the men who are members, others come on their own, and many bring other women to join them as well. Some smoke cigars, some smoke cigarettes, and some don't smoke at all. These ladies join us for the spirits selections we regularly offer at these events or just because they enjoy the networking and find benefits in attending. The CNBMG has a large following of women on social media as well.

There are also a good number of social groups in our area (and on social media) that are headed by women and whose members are mostly women and are also cigar themed. I know many of these women, and they enjoy cigars and are just as passionate about them and their group as I am. So to the ladies reading my book, if you decide to build your own networking group around whatever your hobby or passion may be, I salute you and would encourage you to do so!

Now, as you share all of this with your members and new ambassadors, your vision will become more clear and focused.

Make your vision your mission statement. Write it down. Share it with your group members. Include it in all your correspondence.

Here is our mission statement for the Cigar Night Business Mixer Group:

Our purpose is to encourage and support other like-minded business professionals, business owners and entrepreneurs looking to grow thriving businesses through personal introductions and quality networking, while sharing our enjoyment of great company and a good cigar. Our goal is for all of our members to have 'A Smokin' Networking Experience'!

Yes, in the beginning it will be a numbers game to build a core membership, and yes, you will attract those not quite suited for the group or those who don't meet your standards.

But—and this is an important but—you and your team need to follow through and maintain your high standards, even if that means occasions where a new guest is talked with about your standards so that they're aware for the next event. Or they may be asked to leave and not invited back. It's your group ... and your standards.

Now having said that, this is also when *you* are in the spotlight! As the host, you need to maintain the standards for your group by example. Remember, *you* are the face of the group, and your members and guests are watching.

One final note. It's very important to let your group know that it's all about them.

The event works because of them. I routinely do that during our formal announcement and introduction session. I simply share with them that our CNBMG networking events are only a success because they themselves are there for each mixer, and I thank them all. In reality, it's true, and I do sincerely mean it.

CHAPTER SIX

SO WHAT'S YOUR PURPOSE?

It's just a job. Grass grows, birds fly, waves pound the sand. I beat people up.

Muhammad Ali

So, can *you* do this? Can you duplicate the formula and build your own business networking group? My answer is yes—if you really want to and can see the benefits. It's not to party, it's not a social hour, it's business.

The major reasons for starting your networking group should be clear and written down. That is your "why." It will keep you motivated, eager, hungry, and on point. Make it your mission statement.

The next step is your passion, your draw, your talking point. It doesn't matter if you're a plumber, a dentist, or a funeral home owner—you can connect your passion and hobby to make it work for you.

Many years back, I had a friend and business acquaintance who owned a mortuary and funeral home. He was witty, enjoyed networking, and was an avid runner. That was his passion—he organized 5 and 10Ks and marathons as a way to network using his passion for running. And his business did very well. He knew everyone and everyone knew him. While thankfully I haven't yet needed his services, to this day I remember his slogan: "Hello, everyone. My name is Joe and I own Joe's Funeral Services where we always promise to let you down easy." That's staying power.

Here is where I want to share my dirty little secret with you! My original title for this book was *Smoking and Drinking Your Way to Business*

Success—One Man's Tale of Successful Smokin' Business Mixers.

I even came up with some catchy slogans and anagrams: Cigar Networking... Cigars to Clients and Puros to Profits!

Or how about this little gem: C I G A R S

Contact	When you first meet ask if they're a cigar smoker.
Invite	Invite them to the next mixer.
Get to know	Learn more about them, build a relationship.
Ask	Ask questions, let them talk and share.
Reciprocate	Give to get. Can you help them?
Set appointment	Set the appointment to meet for business.

And while I thought the title and slogans pretty much said it all, I decided to run it past a number of people I trusted for some feedback. This group included business consultants I have known for a few years as well as a couple of authors I know who have written a number of books. Their feedback caused me to rethink and create a new title. More than a few discarded titles and two months later, you're holding the book with the chosen title.

You see, while the title seemed clever and edgy to me, it was also limiting, offensive, and negative to others. And while my networking group was successful and worked with a limited and targeted agenda, this book needed broader appeal and acceptance.

Here's why. Just because I chose three politically incorrect hobbies to focus on doesn't mean you should or that others should be excluded from experiencing networking success.

Others who have different hobbies and passions and the desire to found their own networking group should not miss out on the opportunity to learn from the ideas and concepts presented here because they were put off by the title.

If I could build a successful and thriving business networking group based on such nasty, vile, and controversial items as cigars, booze, and guns, the use of a more acceptable hobby should work pretty well for you. Business networking success can and should be an opportunity for everyone.

CAUTION: A Smokin' Point Ahead!

This is where I offer a dram of caution! Since we're on the subject of passions and hobbies, I need to remind you that as you're building your networking group you should always keep your *purpose* in mind—that it's a vehicle to help you attract more prospects, business, and income to build your career. It is *not* your "new job" or "career." You need to keep your bearings so that others don't get you sidetracked.

Here's my brief tale. In the first couple of years of building my CNBMG, I was very active and became known in the cigar circles as a "go to" person and resource. One business in particular that I worked with brought cigars and rollers to corporate events, birthday parties, and weddings and such. I invited them to many of our mixers and also helped promote their business within our sphere of influence. I was so effective that many started to associate me with that particular business. The owners of that business then approached me to help them expand their concept to a wider, national audience. They wanted me to travel for them and do this.

While I was honored that they asked ... and thanked them for their faith in me, I had to politely say no to their offer. As I explained to them, I was *not* in the cigar business. I was in the financial services business. My involvement with cigars (and spirits and firearms) was simply a tool to build my networking machine to help grow my business.

This also made me pause to reflect on how I presented myself in the future to avoid further confusion.

CHAPTER SEVEN

SOCIAL MEDIA:
USING THE "NET" AS *YOUR* NET!

*The richest people in the world
look for and build networks.
Everyone else looks for work.*

Robert Kiyosaki
FOUNDER OF THE RICH DAD COMPANY

So you have your game plan and purpose. Now what? It's time to get even more social! Social media that is.

When it comes to using social media sites to help promote and grow your group, there are many choices available. Our Cigar Night Business Mixer Group has chosen to use Facebook and

LinkedIn as our primary social media forums. Our focus is to share our group and its activities with the world to build recognition and a following and also as a tool to attract and invite new members.

On Facebook, our CNBMG currently has two group sites and three page sites. To help build a following and visibility, we continuously post photos with short descriptions about our past mixers and venues on our multiple sites. We then share these with other groups and pages that share our passion for cigars or spirits and networking.

A few of these sites are either outside of California or out of the country. We have "friends" and "likes" from Italy, Australia, countries in South America, and more. While these out-of-the- area Facebook friends cannot attend one of our events, they do share an appreciation for our passions and post their comments, stories, and photos.

We also share our mixer event photos, as well as invitations to our mixers with industries that would complement and contribute to our group's agenda. These are cigar vendors and manufacturers, spirits representatives, and distillers as well as craft brewers and wine distributers. These postings help expand our group's recognition and credibility and give us a global presence.

The second use of our Facebook sites is as a tool to invite those friends who we believe would appreciate, enjoy, and add value to our mixers. We do this using the "event" app on our Facebook sites and have found it to be effective and very simple to use. We simply create our event and share it with selected sites. We also send out invitations to friends of our sites to join us.

I should mention that we don't use "sponsored" posts or paid promotions. We want to control our postings and not blast them to thousands of people who may not be a fit for our group. Another issue I have heard about recently is that Facebook is looking more and more into controlling the content being distributed through its platform. I'm happy to say that to date I haven't experienced any issues in this area.

Now moving on to our use of LinkedIn. Since LinkedIn is generally considered a more professional and business-oriented forum, my posting there uses a more formal tone.

I select specific groups in the professions that I believe are complementary to mine in the financial services arena. I also select sites on LinkedIn that I believe my target prospect would frequent. And finally I choose sites that I believe will attract the quality members who will bring benefits and value to our group.

The posts on LinkedIn are also usually in two forms as well. The first is a more abbreviated and formal invitation to our upcoming mixer that is posted and shared with the target sites and their members. This invitation includes our mission statement as well so the viewer will know up-front the purpose and theme of our networking mixer. This avoids any confusion.

The benefit of this type of post for me professionally is that the reader will usually check out my LinkedIn profile and learn about what I do and inquire via a LinkedIn message. It offers me a way to "promote" myself as a side note since such self-promotion is frowned upon in my industry.

The second form of posting is the use of a business or industry-related article that would be of interest to the targeted LinkedIn group and its members. Here I do *not* mention our networking group. But what usually happens is that the reader will check out my profile and see that along with my financial industry information, I'm also the founder of a cigar-related networking group. And again, if there is interest, they can connect with me.

Rarely does a week pass that I don't receive an inquiry from these postings requesting more information about my financial offerings or our Cigar Mixer group.

While these two social media sites work well for me and our CNBMG networking format, it certainly doesn't mean others couldn't or wouldn't work. I encourage you to experiment and find what works best for you.

CHAPTER EIGHT

THE OTHER SECRET

People don't buy goods and services.
They buy relations, stories, and magic.

Seth Godin
AUTHOR AND BUSINESSMAN

At this point, I need to share with you that I believe I can, through these pages, help you on your journey to more and better business, with a lot of fun along the way.

Okay, here's the secret. Are you ready?

We rarely talk business at these mixers.

Sure, we know it's about building our businesses. That's why we're there. Yet the tone set by the organizer and format creates a more casual, fun, conversational, and shared interest ambiance so that you tend to talk business at a later time, almost as an afterthought. It feels more like a secondary goal and a very natural thing to do.

We share stories about our shared passions (cigars, Scotch, cars, firearms, fishing, sports, etc.), which then help grow and build relationships, familiarity, and trust. We're smoking cigars, enjoying our libations, smiling, and laughing.

So how does this help grow your business? It sounds like a party, right? Well, it is—a party with a purpose!

At the end of those conversations or the end of our mixers, it's a natural segue into, "Hey, I really enjoyed talking with you. I'd like to meet in the next few days and learn more about what you do and share a bit about what I do and see if we can collaborate down the road."

At this point, "yes" is almost always the answer. This happens over and over at our mixers.

I usually leave with three to five contacts that I need to call the next day to set up a meeting with. And these are people I *want* to meet with and build a relationship with—and do business with!

Here's food for thought. It has been said that most big business deals happen not in the boardroom but on the golf course or the private country club, especially in major cities.

Why? A shared interest, shared passion, no pressure, and no sales agenda. These are the places where relationships are built and deals follow.

But wait! You don't play golf or belong to a county club or private club? How are you supposed to meet these people to start building those relationships? The answer is simpler than you might think. You get yourself invited! But remember, you won't have a chance if you're the typical salesperson looking for that next deal now.

Simply put—people don't want to be "sold." The sales tactics of the "Wolf of Wall Street" era of the 80s and 90s just don't cut it any more. And after the 2008 market crash, people are scared, wary, and downright hostile when it comes to being pushed into a sale—and with good reason. Stocks, bonds, commodities, and foreign markets all took a beating. Even contrarian and safe haven areas like gold and real estate weren't spared. Many investors lost a third to a half or more of their wealth over a seventeen-month period. Can you blame them for being cautious and skeptical or wanting to aggressively protect what wealth they had left? This includes the ultra-wealthy as well as the upper middle class and average investors with their IRAs.

So my point: don't be like all the other salespeople out there. Think outside the box. Or better yet, build a better box!

Here's an example of blending your passion with business networking. One of my good friends and business associates, Sergey Molkov, had been a part of my newly formed Cigar Night Business Mixer Group and took the idea one step further. Combining his enjoyment of a good cigar with his hobby of being a firearms enthusiast (as a former Russian military guy!), he created a "Client Appreciation Day at the Gun Range" as a way to thank current clients and meet new prospects that the clients brought. He then created his *Cigars and Guns* Facebook page to promote and post pictures of the gun range outings. As of this writing, it has been a six-year success.

That's thinking outside the box. Or, you could say, creating a whole new box!

CHAPTER NINE

AH, TO THE CONTRARY!

*The reasonable man adapts himself to the
conditions that surround him.
The unreasonable man adapts surrounding
conditions to himself. All progress depends
on the unreasonable man.*

George Bernard Shaw
IRISH PLAYWRIGHT

I was interviewed by a regional business
journal a while back and asked why I chose
alternative investments as a career path. My
answer, after a moment to reflect, was that I had
always been contrarian in nature. And as a light
student of history, I saw many occasions where

success was achieved through contrarian means. While I won't dwell on that in this book, I would encourage you to do some research yourself. Fascinating!

As I've mentioned, in California where I live, I chose to build my business networking group around three of my hobbies/passions that are all very non-politically correct, controversial, and notoriously evil: cigars, spirits, and guns! *Yikes!*

Yet despite these unconventional anchors, our group has grown and flourished. We have contacts across the nation and around the globe. We are discussed, friend-ed, connected, texted, and chatted with by many thousands who share our enjoyment of and passion for a premium cigar, premium spirit, and well-tooled and accurate firearm.

What I didn't fully realize when I and our original eight members sat around pitching each other ideas on what our new networking group would look like or who our target market was and what the hook would be to bring in the quality of members we needed was the vast number of people who enjoy the same passion for our chosen themes of cigars, spirits, and firearms.

Then, as I looked through the entertainment, sports, society, luxury lifestyle, and business publications that my ideal prospect—wealthy, successful, and affluent individuals—would likely subscribe to, I started to notice a common theme of big game hunting, exclusive golf resorts and vacation sites, ultra-premium spirits, and high-end cigars. Maybe because these were also my hobbies and passions as well they seemed to speak to me—here is my prospect and this is their lifestyle.

While the Cigars and Guns group developed a year or so after our original cigars and spirits-focused group was founded, it was a natural offshoot (pun intended!) for our members and was a success from the beginning.

So, what does this all mean? It means be bold, be unique, be contrarian. Stand out. Don't be afraid to experiment!

Why? Well, quite honestly, cigar gatherings and wine tastings and spirits tasting groups have been around for decades. What I and our CNBMG members did was simply add the business networking component and bam! These gatherings took on a whole new aura.

At our monthly CNBMG networking events, it has become a regular occurrence for someone to come up to me during the evening and tell me how "unique and comfortable" this mixer was and thank me for organizing it. And a good number of those attending our mixers on a regular basis have told me that they have or would skip an industry event if on the same day to attend our business mixer. Many say they want to invite friends and co-workers and even their supervisor or boss to our mixer as well. To me, that shows value and a healthy business and social atmosphere.

Think about it again. Mixers aren't new. Cigars and spirits aren't new. Bringing them together with a purpose was my breakthrough moment. And that purpose was made part of our networking group's name—the Cigar Night Business Mixer Group.

It's also emphasized in our brief ten to fifteen-minute "formal" session where our introductions and announcements are made. We all know it's a business networking event.

Yes, these *are* social events. Yes, we are sharing cigar, firearms, and spirits stories and trivia in a very casual and relaxed environment. But it's also about being focused and being in sales and networking mode and building relationships— all with the purpose of creating more business.

CHAPTER TEN

THE BUCKS STOP HERE

Someone has to do it. Why not me?

Unknown

No, that is not a typo. The *bucks* should stop with you, in the form of more qualified warm prospects and more business.

In almost every industry, a steady stream of new and qualified prospects is the illusive holy grail. So much so that many spend hundreds or thousands of dollars sourcing and/or buying "qualified" leads lists. Others spend big money hosting seminars and workshops to attract potential prospects and clients for their product or service. Now if you have a big budget and want to go that direction, that's fine. But if you're a small business owner or consultant or independent agent like I am and many others in the financial industry are, it can be a challenge to compete with the big hitters out there on a smaller or limited budget. You have to be creative to get the most bang for your buck.

I believe being the head of your own networking group can help achieve your goal of more prospects, more market reach, and more business. Being the founder of my own networking group is a total rush. It puts me in a unique and rewarding position. I control the quantity and quality of the membership. I become the guy people need to meet. There is also a residual benefit to being the leader of your own networking group. You get to help others in your group to connect and grow their network and business.

Now before you start thinking, "Wow, this John guy has a big ego and a big head," let me share this with you. I'm grateful and humbled by the way the Cigar Night Business Mixer Group has grown, and the quality people who are part of our membership. I never forget that *they* make it happen. *They* make it work. *They* make it successful. And I thank them always for that.

You see, what gets my motor running, besides adding a new client to my business, is having someone that I connected with someone else in the group call me up and tell me that they met last week and are doing business together. That's exciting. That means our group is working!

Furthermore, I believe it shines a positive light on you: you're the connector, the one who helps make things happen and cares about your members' success as well as your own.

I get a couple of calls or emails a week from group members introducing me to a new member that they're bringing to the next mixer. Or I'll receive a call from a member who wants to meet "the well dressed, tall guy who's a commercial real estate broker" that they met at our mixer but then lost their business card. (Important note: Don't lose their business card!) When you become the "go to" person, it's a very special and exciting position.

Here's a quick example of how being the founder of your own networking group can help you connect with more warm prospects. I send out email invitations for our networking mixers regularly. Occasionally one will come back as undelivered. I use this as an occasion to call the person and get their new email address and set up a time to meet and catch up—and of course talk with them about what I do.

And the beauty of all of this "connecting" is that it gives me the opportunity to talk about my business, every time!

I know that my building of the CNBMG has personally worked for me. I would say that I could directly attribute about two-thirds of my new business over the last few years directly to the group and the networking activity. In addition, there are a good number of members who have made great connections as well and generated new prospects, clients, and business. That's why I believe they keep attending!

CHAPTER ELEVEN

IT'S NOT WHAT YOU KNOW BUT WHO KNOWS YOU

*It isn't just what you know, and it isn't just who you know.
It's actually who you know, who knows you, and what you do for a living.*

Bob Burg
AUTHOR OF *ENDLESS REFERRALS* AND *THE GO-GIVER*

As I've mentioned, being the founder of your own networking group has many perks. You get to build your networking group the way you want in order to target your type of prospect.

For me these were positive, successful, business-oriented professionals who were in related or complementary fields of business that could potentially introduce me to future prospects and for whom I could do the same in return.

But what I believe is the most exciting perk associated with being the head of your own business networking group is the visibility it gives you.

Here's one example. In 2010, just after founding the CNBMG in February, I was contacted by officials from Orange County and asked if our group would help with their program to raise funds and collect cigars and personal care items to be sent to our troops stationed in Iraq. They had heard about our group from other cigar smokers who frequented the restaurants that the county supervisors and city officials went to for lunches and meetings.

Of course I said yes. And since I was a vintage Corvette owner and enthusiast, I suggested we also invite all the local Corvette clubs and members to participate as well. Almost all said yes unless they had a conflicting event, since many of their members were veterans, cigar smokers, or both.

The event was a huge success. We had more than thirty Corvettes on display that day, ranging from 1953 to 2010 models. We collected enough funds, personal care items, and cigars to send more than 300 pounds of goods to our military personnel in Iraq. The event was attended by many city, county, and state officials as well as hundreds of people who wanted to support our service members. We received widespread media coverage, and afterward our CNBMG group received a beautiful plaque as a thank you from our county supervisor.

What was most exciting and touching was the photo we received a few weeks later from the troops who received the packages—many with big smiles—and a lit cigar planted firmly in that smile!

This charity event not only gave our CNBMG great exposure, it also gave us credibility as a well-organized and caring group that could and would deliver on our commitments. As our group membership expanded from eight attendees to averaging more than fifty per mixer, the occasions when someone would come up to me at a restaurant, cigar lounge, or other event became more frequent. And now, in 2018, with an email membership of more than 2,000 and attendance at our monthly cigar mixers averaging eighty-plus each month at each of our three chapters, hardly a week goes by that someone doesn't come up to me and say, "Hey, aren't you John, the cigar guy?" That's pretty exciting!

Of course I answer "yes" and a conversation ensues and a new opportunity to make a friend and build a relationship over shared interests presents itself. Oh, and this is a new person with whom I can share information about what I do as a financial professional—and who can potentially become a client. Wow!

One of the first special event invitations I received was to a private reception where former President of Mexico Vicente Fox was to speak. Due to a business conflict, I couldn't make it to the event. However, I did connect with his people a few days later and since I knew he was a fellow cigar smoker, I arranged for President Fox to be interviewed for a major cigar publication. So, while I may not have gained a new client, it was because I was the founder of the CNBMG that the invitation to these events was extended to me, which was a great perk and would never have occurred otherwise.

CHAPTER TWELVE

THE PERKS

There is a very real relationship, both quantitatively and qualitatively, between what you contribute and what you get out of this world.

Oscar Hammerstein II
SONGWRITER

I could probably write a separate book on this subject alone. First, a little personal background.

As a kid I grew up fairly poor and in a fractured family. I never went to the same elementary school in any of my kindergarten through sixth grade years. We were always moving, due to either eviction or because rents were raised and we couldn't afford to stay. We never owned a home or a decent car ... when we had a car at all!

That lack of stability—constantly leaving one place and not knowing how long I would be in the new one—led me to be a very closed person. I didn't make friends easily and being in social situations was uncomfortable for me. I barely made it out of high school and didn't have the funds or the desire to go to college.

I did have a work ethic, though. No friends ... and no social events ... left me plenty of time to work! That, and I certainly needed the money.

My working whenever I could also served me well as I moved out at seventeen and started life on my own. I'm grateful for the experiences and opportunities I had in my teens and late twenties that brought me some level of success and a good income. That came mostly while I was in the restaurant industry from my early twenties to my late thirties. That's where I developed my social and people skills.

I would recommend working six months to a year in a service industry for everyone early on in their career. It's a great training ground.

I then discovered the sales profession, and my life changed. As a licensed financial professional, I learned early on that building relationships—not "selling"—was the key to success. Fortunately, my years in the restaurant business helped me greatly in this area. That was the reasoning behind the founding of my CNBMG—to build relationships.

As the CNBMG grew in membership and visibility, the group became recognized as a "go to" networking event. And as the group grew, so did the perks!

In the beginning, it was the small things, such as never having to make another cold call. Then as we grew, it was being offered free cigars and bottles of spirits and wines by manufacturers' reps who wanted to sponsor our mixers.

I've been interviewed by a newspaper columnist; asked to write for a well-known cigar publication; met and interviewed cigar legends, movie and TV stars, and business and sports greats; and invited to host cigar events at exclusive private clubs. All this simply because I founded a networking group built around my passion for and enjoyment of a premium cigar and a fine-aged spirit.

As our CNBMG grew, I began receiving invitations and free tickets to many exclusive and upscale events where I was able to mingle with the "who's who" of the region and share my CNBMG stories and invite them to join us at the next mixer.

Many of these events were held at private clubs such as the Grand Havana Room in Beverly Hills, the Center Club Orange County, and the City Club Los Angeles, and at exclusive golf resorts like Coto de Caza and Morgan Run.

Attending these events, I would meet well-known movers and shakers like Carl Nolet, Jr. of Ketel One and Nolet's Gin; Arnold Schwarzenegger; Peter Weller; and Cedric the

Entertainer; and I've even shared a cigar with William Shatner.

So, while I may not have gained a new client at the time, it was because I was the founder of the CNBMG that the invitation to these events was extended to me, which was a great perk and would never have occurred otherwise.

Another invitation sent my way was to an event called the Gentleman's Smoker and Charity Gala that was held at the Balboa Bay Club in Newport Beach, California. Once again, I was unable to attend due to a previous business commitment with a client (which always comes first!) on the same night.

It was fortunate, however, that one of our CNBMG members who was also invited did attend. At that event he happened to meet the CEO of a start-up magazine. The next day, the member called me and suggested I meet the CEO as he was very interested in our group. At that time, our group was only about a year old but getting a lot of attention in the area. I called the magazine that same day and set up a meeting, which went very well. I offered to help promote the magazine at our mixers and through our social media connections. I also invited the CEO to join us at any of our mixers to promote his magazine. In return, he offered to give me a few subscriptions to raffle off. The events went very well, and he made some good contacts as well.

A few months later, I was offered the opportunity to write articles for the magazine about cigar and spirits pairings. I also contacted and interviewed the owners of well-known cigar and spirits brands and those interviews were published in his cigar magazine. This collaboration opened up many doors for me as the magazine grew and flourished.

Today, that CEO and publisher, Lincoln Salazar, heads up the very successful *Cigar & Spirits Magazine* empire that has worldwide readership. I consider myself fortunate to count Lincoln as a great friend and fellow cigar enthusiast, a connection that was a direct result of my being the founder of the Cigar Night Business Mixer Group.

I will mention that I did finally get to attend the Gentleman's Smoker event the next year. I've attended the following years as well and have always had a great time and met many great people. A good number wound up becoming CNBMG members. And, of course, a few became clients!

Today, the perks just keep coming. Because of my CNBMG reputation in the spirits, cigar, and business arenas, I've met and made friends with very successful people in the financial and hotel industries, as well as in entertainment and politics. I still receive many invitations (many at no cost) to exclusive events and private clubs in the region that I wouldn't have had access to otherwise.

All of these invitations place me right in the middle of my target group's world!

CHAPTER THIRTEEN

THE FINALE

*Every ending is a beginning. We just
don't know it at the time.*

Mitch Albom
AUTHOR AND JOURNALIST

Well, here we are, the finale. It's been
exciting for me to share my thoughts and
experiences regarding business networking, and
I hope you found the ideas presented thought
provoking. The whole focus of my book has been
to encourage you to consider starting your own
business networking group if you believe it would
benefit you and your career.

In addition, I wanted to share a blueprint for your own networking group so you could enjoy the business growth and success that can come with it.

Yes, I had my challenges. Yes, it took a bit of work before the CNBMG took off and started to grow organically and take on a life of its own. But every day I'm thankful for the spark that started it all and those beginning members who supported me and hung in there as we went through our growing pains when only eight or nine people showed up.

I'm also grateful for all those I met along the way who helped promote the group, spread the word, and invited their friends, business associates, and coworkers to join us.

And a sincere thank you to those who helped scout and secure our venues and who reached out to vendors to sponsor our mixers. Also, thanks to the venue owners and managers who took a chance and offered a location to host our mixers at no charge.

And a big thanks to the many industry vendors who hosted spirits tastings, donated product and merchandise, cigars, spirits, raffle prizes, food, and gift certificates, even when we had only fifteen to twenty people show up.

I'm also *very* thankful for my patient and understanding wife who supported me in the early months even though she just *knew* I was only "drinking, smoking cigars, and partying!" I hope I've rewarded her patience.

And finally, I want to thank you, the reader, for taking the time to read this. I appreciate you allowing me to share my thoughts and success with you.

My challenge to you now is to get going. Start planning and brainstorming. Start on your own path to more clients and more business success. Become the "go to" person in your world and reap the benefits of being your own center of influence.

It's time to get your ... Networking Net Working!

Wishing you an awesome journey.

Cheers,

John Dade
Founder of the Cigar Night Business Mixer Group
877-331-2533
John@CigarNightBizMixer.com

Your opinion and feedback is important to me and encouraged. I look forward to your further questions and inquiries.

EIGHT QUESTIONS
YOU NEED TO ASK YOURSELF

1. Do you need more business and income?
    Yes___ No____
2. Do you need to meet more of your target
    prospects? Yes___ No___
3. Do you enjoy cold calling or the prospecting
    activities you're doing now? Yes___ No___
4. Do you enjoy networking?
    Yes___ No___
5. Are your current networking activities as
    productive as you would like them to be?
    Yes___ No___
6. Are you very good at what you do as a
    profession? Yes___ No___
7. Are you open to creating and being your
    own center of influence? Yes___ No___
8. Are you worth it? Yes___ No___

ABOUT THE AUTHOR

John R. Dade is a successful Financial Services Professional with over 15 years of experience in that industry. John has both a Series 3 and a Series 65 license and specializes in "Alternative Investments".

John credits part of his success in the financial arena to his previous 18-year career in the restaurant industry where he learned his customer service skills from the ground up. Starting as a cook, John honed those skill as he moved quickly forward to management then on to a VP position before becoming a 2 unit franchise owner for a well-known pizza chain.

When he transitioned to the financial arena in 1989 he had some success early on but knew there had to be a better way to reach his target market.

This led to his starting up his unique business networking group centered around his passion for Fine Cigars, Premium Spirits and recreational Firearms outings.

The Cigar Night Business Mixer Group was founded in 2010 and it is based in Southern California.

With the growth and success of his Cigar Night Business Mixer Group networking format more than a few members suggested that he write a book and share the details and success with others needing to network and expand their careers.

John lives with his wife Lydia in Orange County California and has one son who is married with two children and lives in San Juan Capistrano CA .

Morgan James
Speakers Group

www.TheMorganJamesSpeakersGroup.com

We connect Morgan James published authors with live and online events and audiences who will benefit from their expertise.